Contents

 Fiction
The Giant Eagle's Feather
page 2

 **Non-fiction**
Raptors
page 14

Written by
Alison Hawes

Illustrated by
Ollie Cuthbertson

Series editor **Dee Reid**

Part of Pearson

Before reading: THE GIANT EAGLE'S FEATHER

Characters

 Salan

 The King

 The Giant Eagle

 Giant Eagle Chicks

Tricky words

- feather
- huge
- talons
- afraid
- attack
- bleeding
- shadow
- swoops

Read these words to the student. Help them with these words when they appear in the text.

Introduction

Salan is a slave. He wants to be free. But the evil King will only grant Salan his freedom if he can do four difficult and dangerous tasks.

One of Salan's tasks is to find the Giant Eagle and take one of its huge feathers back to the King.

THE GIANT EAGLE'S FEATHER

Salan wants to be free. But first he must find a Giant Eagle's feather and take it to the King.

Salan sees a Giant Eagle. It is so big!
It has huge talons and a sharp beak.
Salan is afraid it will attack him.

Salan has a plan.
He climbs up to the eagle's nest to look for a feather.

He is in luck.
There is a huge feather in the nest.
But there are huge chicks in the nest too!

As Salan picks up the feather, the chicks attack him.
They peck at him with their sharp beaks and dig their sharp talons into his hands.

Salan is bleeding.
But he has the feather in his hand!
But then Salan sees a huge shadow.
It is the eagle.
The eagle swoops down and picks up Salan by his hair.

Salan is afraid the eagle will drop him on to the rocks below.

But then Salan sees a tree below him.
He grabs his sword and cuts his hair free.

Down and down he falls.

But as Salan falls, he grabs at the tree below him.
He does not fall on to the rocks.

Salan is bleeding but he has the eagle's feather in his hand!

Salan will take the feather to the King.
Then soon, he will be free.

Quiz

Text comprehension

Literal comprehension
p5 What is Salan's plan?
p6 Why is Salan in luck?

Inferential comprehension
p6 Do you think Salan's plan to climb up to the nest works well?
p9 What do you think would happen if the Giant Eagle dropped Salan on the rocks?
p10 Why does Salan cut off his hair?

Personal response
- Which do you think is Salan's best plan: climbing up to the nest or cutting off his hair? Why?
- What plan could you come up with to get a feather from a Giant Eagle?

Word knowledge

p4 Find four adjectives on this page.
p7 Find four plurals on this page.
p11 Which conjunction joins two parts of the final sentence on this page?

Spelling challenge

Read these words:

must   **look**   **there**

Now try to spell them!

Ha! Ha! Ha!

What bird is always out of breath?

A puffin!

Before reading RAPTORS

Find out about

- how raptors use five deadly weapons to kill their prey.

Tricky words

- raptors
- machines
- use
- deadly
- weapons
- prey
- feathers
- talons

Read these words to the student. Help them with these words when they appear in the text.

Introduction

Birds of prey are called raptors. They are like killing machines in the sky. They use their good hearing, good eyesight, sharp talons, sharp beaks and strong wings to hunt out and swoop down on their prey.

Raptors

Raptors are killing machines.
They rule the sky!
They use five deadly weapons
to hunt down their prey.

Ears

Raptors have very good hearing. Their ears are hidden in their feathers, but they still have good hearing.

Some raptors hunt at night. They use their good hearing to find their prey.

Eyes

Raptors can see very well.
Their feathers cover part of their eyes so they don't look big, but some raptors can see their prey a mile away!

Feet

Raptors have sharp talons on their feet.
They are deadly weapons.
Most raptors use their talons to kill their prey.
But some raptors use their talons to knock their prey out of the sky!

Some raptors have talons like fish-hooks.
They swoop down and use their talons to catch fish.

Beaks

Raptors have sharp beaks. Most raptors use their beaks to cut up their prey.

But some raptors use their beaks to kill their prey.
They have a tooth in their beak.
They use this tooth to snap the neck of their prey.

Wings

Raptors can fly very fast.
They can fly and not make any noise.
They swoop down and catch their prey.

Raptors are killing machines.
They use their ears, eyes, feet, beaks and wings to kill their prey.
They rule the sky!

Quiz

Text comprehension

Literal comprehension
p16 Why is it surprising that raptors have good hearing?
p20–21 How do different raptors use their beaks?

Inferential comprehension
p16 Why is good hearing useful for raptors hunting at night?
p22 Why is flying without making any noise useful for the raptor?
p23 Why are raptors called 'killing machines'?

Personal response
- Have you ever seen a bird of prey? Did you think it was scary?
- What deadly weapons do you think a leopard uses to hunt down its prey?

Word knowledge

p17 Which two words are contracted in 'don't'?
p18 Find a word with a silent letter at the beginning.
p23 Think of a suitable heading for this page.

Spelling challenge

Read these words:

see   away   they

Now try to spell them!

Ha! Ha! Ha!

Why do birds fly south for the winter?

Because it's too far to walk.